MW01644835

Life Lessons by
Titan

as told to

Melaney Taylor Auxier

For Olivia

In memory of
Titan

Support your local
animal shelter

Hi, I'm Titan and this is my story.

love

I used to be sad and stinky
until my new human rescued me.
She washed me and
brushed me until I was clean.

She fell in love instantly
because I'm so lovable.
I'm also very grateful.
I think I'll keep her.

At first, new things were kinda scary,
like stairs.
A nice box fort made me feel safe.

Mistakes can be embarrassing
but that's how we learn.

It's important to take a moment
to have a sit and
think things through.

Trying a different perspective
helps when things are hard to understand.

Sometimes you just need to chill.

Take a moment to smell the flowers.
Your nose might tickle
but it always makes me happy.

Eat healthy food for a healthy body.

Get plenty of rest.
There's nothing wrong with a little nap now and then.

Big or small, it's nice to have
a couple close friends
just to hang out with
and tell a few jokes.

A hearty laugh
is good for the soul.

It's amazing what a little hug can do for your mood.
It's a comforting way to show,
'I got you.'

Remember to say your prayers,
and always be thankful.

No matter
what kind of day it was,
look forward to
the blessings
tomorrow will bring.

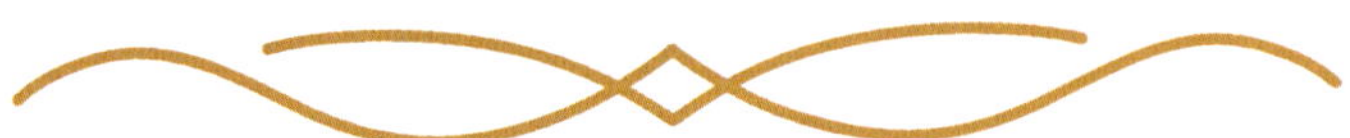

Little Willow Press
2024

Made in the USA
Middletown, DE
04 July 2024

56814246R00022